THE LESS HURRIED PAST

THE LESS HURRIED PAST

Poems for Grace

Roger Averill

© Roger Averill 2019

The moral rights of the authors have been asserted

First published 2019

An urtext book

All rights reserved. No part of this publication may be reproduced or transmitted in any form or by any means, electronic or mechanical, including photocopying, recording or by any information storage retrieval system without permission of Roger Averill, or under terms agreed with the appropriate reprographics rights organization. Enquires concerning reproduction outside the scope of the above should be sent to Roger Averill at the above address.

National Library of Australia Cataloguing-in-Publication Data
A catalogue record for this book is available from the National Library of Australia

Paperback: ISBN: 978-0-9923734-6-7

I am like a tree,
From my top boughs I can see
The footprints that led up to me.

     —R. S. Thomas

For Grace Mallett Averill

CONTENTS

In the Belly of the Moon	11
Five	13
Questions of the Sky	14
Like	15
Instruction	16
Icidy Picidy	19
The Wash	22
The Grade Six Halleluiah	23
Literary Parents	25
Bike Rider's Rap	27
Tyre Tunes	30
The Sing Thing	32
Addendum to Pablo Neruda's *Book of Questions*	34
Lumière d'Hiver	36
Winter Light	37
Journeywork	38
Brae	40
Tulips	41
You	43
The Diary of Amos Boyle	47

IN THE BELLY OF THE MOON

The screen shifted, swam, then suddenly,
like seeing a mermaid in the diaphanous depths,
I saw you, my own child, as yet unborn.

Science conjured and confirmed you
in its own certain image.
The computer's magic measured your skull,
your toothpick limbs;
scanned each organ for fault and deformity.
Your left kidney, dilated.
A tiny blemish on the screen,
it lay dark like cloud-shadow across my thoughts.
The sonagrapher did not panic.
Pushing buttons, changing angles,
adjusting the focus—
still, she could not be sure.
The doctor deliberated, for a moment:
a lifetime.
'The upper end of normal,' he mumbled,
staring at the monitor, ignoring your mother,
prostrate on the bed.
'It may right itself.'

Fingers furled into a fist, mouth open—
a yawn? a scream?—
you wriggled in and out of focus,
bones to flesh, then back to bone.
How strange that my first glimpse
of you was of your skeleton.
It didn't seem right, the natural order inverted.
With luck, I will know you forever,
as long as my ever lasts,
and it will be you who buries my bones
or casts them as ash upon the sea.

For now, though, all I hold is hope
and an image of you floating in your mother's womb.
The plastic slide lifted to the light,
your profile remains only the suggestion
of a grainy silhouette.
Still a mystery, a possibility,
you are like the man half-seen sleeping
in the full belly of the moon.

February 1998

FIVE

I can't believe it, it can't be true—
I remember when you were only two.
I never thought this day would arrive,
But here it is, and now you're five.

Years ago, when you'd just turned three,
I thought you were as big as a girl could be.
Then three hundred and sixty-five days sped by,
And suddenly you were four and twice as high.

So now the moon has circled us twelve times more,
You're older and wiser than ever before.
But time will continue to play its tricks
And the next thing I'll know you'll be turning six.

July 2003

QUESTIONS OF THE SKY

When you were two or three, still very young,
You looked up at the sky
And, shielding your eyes against the sun,
Asked, 'Dad, why must we die?'

Then one night, staring at the moon,
You said you thought it a plastic bag,
Floating there like a child's balloon;
The cloud beside it, a scrap of rag.

Another time, when the sky was completely dark
—Except of course for a few billion stars—
You said the night was a spotted dog about to bark
At planes and satellites, like passing cars.

Looking now at the sky where it touches the sea,
Seeing the sun skip over the depths below,
You turn and ask, 'Dad, how did I get to be me?'
And all I can say is, 'I really don't know.'

One thing, however, I'm certain is true,
As you grow older—now turning seven—
I'll always be standing right beside you,
Whenever you gaze at the mysteries of heaven.

July 2005

LIKE

When girls in Brunswick reach a certain age
They develop a habit that's all the rage.

Reading chapter books and riding a bike,
All their sentences suddenly start with 'like'.
For example, one of them might happen to say,
'Like, these other kids came, so like I ran away'.

It's not that they're fond of this likable word,
The attraction's more mysterious, even absurd.
It's more of an illness, something they catch,
A seven year itch they simply must scratch.

But when they turn eight, or so I've been told,
These girls mature; become really quite old.
The way that they talk changes overnight,
'Like' disappears and everything's just 'right'.

Right?

July 2006

INSTRUCTION

Whatever I do, my parents tell me how.
'Do it this way,' they say, 'Not later, now!'

Dad, I gather, played netball for Australia
—Keeper, Shooter, Wing Attack—
Mum took tea with the Queen in full regalia,
Pinky crooked for the royal snack.
In his younger days, Dad played piano with exquisite feeling
In all the finest concert halls,
And while Michelangelo painted the Sistine ceiling,
Mum, it seems, did the walls.

I know they mean well, that they're trying to help,
But their words wash over me like waves over kelp.
Read what they say and you'll know what I mean,
Say it over and over and you'll be ready to scream.

>   Sit straight
>   Watch the ball
>   Pick yourself up
>   When you fall
>
>   Grip the pen with
>   Your driver finger

Open your mouth
To be a good singer

Look at the music
Move your feet
Mouth closed
When you eat

Pace yourself
Throw from the shoulder
You'll thank us for this
When you are older

That's "Lily and I"
Not "Lily and me"
Keep your rhythm
Play middle C

Read the notes
Get front position
Look both ways
Use intuition

Arms up
In defence
Remember to relax
And not be tense

Legs down
At the table
Enjoy yourself
While you're able

Use a CAPITAL
When a sentence begins
Smile hearty when
The other side wins

Flat throws
No lollipops
& always remember
The full stops.

So many instructions, they'll drive me barmy.
Living with my parents is like being in the army.

P. S.

Did I fail to mention,
they make me stand to attention
whenever they enter the room?
And if I forget,
with some little regret,
they sweep me outside with a
broom.

July 2007

ICIDY PICIDY

You can't be pernickety if you live in Icidy Picidy,
Because this is a land where everyone lends a hand,
Where all types of creatures sport various types of features,
And everyone gets along as they sing the Icidy song.

Oh we might sound strange
And we might look weird,
But here in Icidy Picidy
There's nothing to be feared.
We love each other
And can think of nothing greater
Than celebrating the birthday
Of our wonderful creator.

Now Dr Chute counts his loot
Inside his bubblegum factory.
While Mr Tin, who's frightfully thin,
Has a brain that runs by battery.

The Wooblies, it's true, work all the day through
But at night they fly by the moon.
Their parents, they worry, if they're not home in a hurry,
That they'll sleep 'til the next afternoon.

Beargrubs in bathtubs, soak their rear hubs
To make their tails unfurl,
But as soon as they're dry, in the flash of an eye,
Their tails spring back to a curl.

It's said that a Spry is awfully shy,
That's why you only see them at night.
But you'd better be quick, 'cause they're terribly slick
And they love to give people a fright.

Oh we might sound strange
And we might look weird,
But here in Icidy Picidy
There's nothing to be feared.
We love each other
And can think of nothing greater
Than celebrating the birthday
Of our wonderful creator.

Confused for a kook, Maroon Bloopaduke
Is actually incredibly smart.
She's discovered a gas and done the maths,
And now powers her car from a fart.

Flubabubas use pencils and rubbers
When rafting down a river.
Pen and ink, they're tempted to drink,
If the quill's not back in its quiver.

Pengoos, in twos, cuddle up in igloos
To see the cold winter out.
Doing nothing by halves, they use their ears as scarves
To avoid a frosty snout.

The tail of a Coplop, shaped like a paddlepop,
Is why they can't touch their toes.
But it doesn't explain their sense of pain
At having never been given a nose.

Oh we might sound strange
And we might look weird,
But here in Icidy Picidy
There's nothing to be feared.
We love each other
And can think of nothing greater
Than celebrating the birthday
Of our wonderful creator.

July 2008

THE WASH

Yesterday, pegging your blue Explorer socks to the line,
I saw the ghost of your infant feet, now grown,
marching towards the paling fence.
Kicking out against their tether,
billowed by a sudden breeze,
they floated through the branches of the almond tree,
and, performing a pirouette,
twirled toward the bright winter sky.

July 2009

THE GRADE SIX HALLELUIAH

Now we've heard there is a secret board
On which our Nap tests have been scored,
But you don't really care for schoolin', do ya?
It goes like this, grades prep to six,
The junior school, the senior shift,
The baffled kids composing halleluiah.

Halleluiah, halleluiah,
Halleluiah, halleluiah.

Now baby I've been here before,
I've sat in this class, and I've walked this floor;
I was the fruit monitor before ya.
I gave you apples and a pear,
But all I got were nits in my hair.
It's a red and it's a scratchy halleluiah.

Halleluiah, halleluiah,
Halleluiah, halleluiah.

You love the fete, but you had a bad tooth,
The fairy floss and the lollie jar booth,
The giant slide, it nearly overthrew ya.

So much fun was hard to bear,
More than a good ol' country fair,
And from your lips the dentist drew halleluiah.

Halleluiah, halleluiah,
Halleluiah, halleluiah.

Now maybe there's a life beyond
These walls of which we are so fond,
But we didn't come here just to fool ya.
It's not a cry you'll hear at night,
It's more our laughter as we take flight,
It's sad and it's a joyful halleluiah.

Halleluiah, halleluiah,
Halleluiah, halleluiah.

With apologies to Leonard, August 2010

LITERARY PARENTS

Have you ever noticed
That in all the best books,
The children are orphans,
Or their parents are crooks?

Obviously that's because
Parents are frightful bores,
Busy making happy homes,
They're always doing chores.

Where's the fun in that,
The adventure, the lark?
No, life needs a little tragedy
If a story's to have a spark.

If Anne's folks had all been healthy,
Her family life quite stable,
She never would've become
The famous Anne of Green Gables.

In truth, the secret of Mary's garden
Has nothing to do with a robin.
If her parents hadn't died of cholera,
She'd never have met up with Colin.

If Mrs Hamilton had lived,
Tally would've gone to another school,
She'd never have visited Bergania,
Or discovered the dragonfly pool.

So this, then, is the reason
I'm always highly suspicious
Of a book in which the parents
Aren't dead or horribly vicious.

Which is why I've never read
To Kill a Mocking-bird,
Because the father in it's a hero
—A premise quite absurd.

Perhaps one day I'll read it
(At least the mother's dead),
But it'll be no cinch
Having Atticus Finch
Messing with my head.

July 2010

BIKE RIDER'S RAP

i ain't no fool,
i ride to school.
i prefer to bike it
than bus & hike it.
and seein' me off,
like a butler to a toff,
is poor old dad,
all pyjamas-clad,
rubbin' his eyes and then his mush,
his curly hair like a bramble bush.
with his toes gone cold from the freezin' floor,
he peers out the window, then opens the door,
and seein' that it's rainin',
in the time remainin',
he says to me, his eldest daughter,
"yo, listen up, 'cause you really oughta
pump them brakes,
for heaven's sakes,
'cause rogue car doors
are no respecter of laws,
and as for driveways,
they'll knock ya sideways
—when a car's reversin'

there ain't no rehearsin'."
ridin' off, givin' a wave,
i tried to remember the old man's rave.
it's not that i'm dumb,
just my fingers were numb,
my eyes were streamin',
my mind still dreamin'.
any which ways,
it's safe to says
i was in daze
when a cat in the lane,
rushin' from the rain,
ran across my wheel,
and made me squeal.
after the scream
woke me from my dream
i was fully awake,
and jammed on the brake.
the bike was slidin',
but I kept on ridin',
and the moggy escaped
from our little scrape.
though it wasn't dead,
it must be said,
it had one less paw
than it had before.

what I haven't told dad
so as not to make him mad,
is that i ride by choice
when the roads are moist.
not because i'm some crazy risk-taker
in a burnin' hurry to meet her maker,
it's more about the sound
of the rubber on the ground,
the music you get
when the roads are wet,
as you ride along
and listen to the song
that your tyres sing
as your wheels begin to spin.
i love the beat
from beneath my seat.
the sound of the ground's
sweet symphony,
is the sound unbound
of me bein' free.

July 2011

TYRE TUNES

As inventions go,
Those in the know
Say, with the exception of fire,
There's nothing much higher,
No bigger deal
Than the humble wheel.
Of course, they're referring
To the way that its whirring
Lightens our load
On life's long twisting road.

But me, I'm more impressed
By the way when it's dressed
With a frame
And a chain,
A saddle and the rest,
That it makes me feel free,
Like a sailor at sea,
To simply be me.

The push of my pedal
On this steed made of metal
Is an effort rewarded
—One hereby recorded—
Elevating my soul

To the top of a knoll,
It then hurtles me down
To leveller ground.
Like a skier without snow,
An arrow loosed from a bow,
I fly through the air
With the wind in my hair,
(Or at least in my face
'cause the helmet's in case
Fate schedules a meeting
That entails my unseating).

The sound of the tread
Is a hymn in my head,
A song sung so sweet
On a path or a street.
The shushing refrain
That comes after rain,
A rhythm, a beat,
In the pulsing heat,
A satisfied sigh
When the road becomes dry.
The sound of a tyre
Is my freedom's desire,
A symphony of motion
On an asphalted ocean.

July 2012

THE SING THING

okay, grace, here's the thing,
you don't need to be a bird
to know how to sing.
watch out, though,
don't do it for dough,
'cause the shysters'll pretend
they're cuttin' you a break
but then in the end,
you can guarantee,
it'll only be
for their bank account's sake.
they'll put you down a mine
where the sun don't shine
& try to keep you there
in the stale air
till the end of time.
they'll say it's for some kinda early warnin',
but we've been yellin' "fire!" since
dawn's first mornin'.
the world's a mess,
that much we know,
the bible says we're gonna reap
what we sow.
it might sound strange,

even absurd,
but your lack of feathers don't stop ya
bein' a bird!
so learn to fly, stretch your wing,
& wherever you perch don't forget to sing.
i'm not sayin' that'll turn things round,
only that the world's a better place
when it hears your sound.

July 2013

ADDENDUM TO PABLO NERUDA'S *BOOK OF QUESTIONS*

why does the night forget the day,
shocked anew by the dawn's first ray?

where is that baby I nestled and nursed?
alive in the memory of time's cruel curse?

is the hunt of the hound always pursued by the fox?
could time be stilled if we destroyed all the clocks?

why does the ocean chuckle with laughter,
then roar and hiss only hours after?

how do trees experience birds,
their scratchy feet, their warbled words?

why is the truth not tied in a box
instead of the tangle of a paradox?

what if we hoped for what we believed?
can we be wise and still be deceived?

is to question the answer to answer the question?
is that really our only or our best suggestion?

was the big bang a whimper, after all,
if no one was there to hear its call?

what of the dreams lost to the night,
books composed for those without sight,

libraries of texts without any words,
songs that are sung but are never heard?

is childhood lost, or something we leave,
when we forget how to make believe?

can a memory last, a moment linger,
like the taste of touch on a blind man's finger?

July 2014

LUMIÈRE D'HIVER

La lumière d'hiver reluit
sur les feuilles vert amande
et le vent du nord
les fait frémir

en silencieux applaudissement.

Traduit de l'anglais par Catherine de Saint Phalle, Juillet 2015

WINTER LIGHT

Winter light gleams
the green almond leaves
and the north wind
makes them flutter

in silent applause.

July 2015

JOURNEYWORK

I believe a leaf of grass is no less than the journeywork of the stars

—Walt Whitman

In all its rough-barked beauty,
the elm remains unmoved
by our passing.
Your eighteen years
—*magnificent, momentous*—
etched in the rings
of the tree's
less hurried past,
barely riffle its leaves
in the gentle breeze
of arboreal time.

More grass than trees,
our slender lives,
like blades of green,
slice through the earth
and into time,
their sweetest sap
coursing toward the sun.
Unworried by the cow's

impending lips,
its wrenching teeth,
we think only of the warmth
and of the milk we will become.

July 2016

BRAE (Celtic – *hilltop*)

A cowl of cloud
Hooded your face,
Fuming your sides,
Smoking the valley below.
Audacious in my desires,
Greedy even,
I cried, 'Lift! Lift!'
Beseeching the weather gods
To grant me a glimpse
Of your full glory.

Feeling shamanic now,
I watched in wonder
As the mist lightened,
Then left,
Revealing the burdened
Beauty of your brow:
Worried round by wind
And rain,
Creviced, cragged with cairns,
Cloaked in the regal robes of heather.

Inspired by Laggan, written in Berlin, July 2017

TULIPS

The slow-motion dance
of a vase of tulips
seeking the sun:
arching stems
& bustled skirts
twirling
imperceptibly toward
the dinning room window.

Then, at night,
as if abashed
by such pagan ways
of worship,
they repent & turn
inward,
covering their stamen
shame in darkness.

Heads bowed
by the weight
of time,
their petalled lips
curl
in anguish,
in ecstacy.

Resigned, sun-soaked,
each petal now seems
its own source
of translucent light.
Broken
fully open,
released from all
Edenic guilt,
their curved rays
swoop,
flutter,
& finally float
onto the waiting table-top.

July 2018

YOU

You,
that wee creature
nestled on my chest
to let your mother sleep
the first night you spent
in Stanley Street.

You,
who frightened decades
from our lives
as your tiny furled fingers
threatened to loosen their grip
on existence.

You,
who showed such pluck
enduring operations
and illness,
making us laugh
even as we felt to cry.

You,
creator god,

linguist of imagined lands,
C.S. Lewis & pneumonia,
loving Sophie's longing
for a Highlands of the mind.

You,
the ferocious cyclist
who never asked
are we there yet
but always pleaded
to peddle further.

You,
the sweet kid
seeing life
from the other's side,
thinking of them,
over-thinking yourself.

You,
with the perfect pitch
bottling up our tears,
all the while knowing
that your voice
uncorked them.

You,
the dedicated student
wanting to understand
and to get the grades,
failing only
in cynicism.

You,
admirer of clouds,
collector of leaves,
the crushed smell
of eucalyptus
releasing memories.

You,
you are all these
but they are not you.
The grain in your wood
does not define the span
of your branches.

You,
Grace,
you are
the tree.

April 2019

THE DIARY OF AMOS BOYLE

23 November 1857

Again, I have not attended to this duty for some
weeks. Life is hard enough in the living without
me spending my nights worrying it over on the
page. I have turned every sod on my claim and have
nothing but blisters and an aching back to show
for it. This past month I have worked Maloney's
battery. For a day or so we were finding half an
ounce a day. Then Maloney took to the grog,
drinking his luck away. By the time he had dried
out, so had the seam. Then yesterday part of the
shaft caved in. I was working the battery up top.
Now that the mud has dried out, the dust on the
diggings is like a London fog; I couldn't see two feet
in front of me. And the cracking of the rocks made
it hard to hear. But then, wiping my brow, letting
the cradle rest a moment, I heard his screaming;
cusses and curses that will surely gain him entry
into Hell. In my hurry to reach him, scrambling
down the embankment, crawling into the shaft,
I forgot to take a lamp. His, it seemed, had been
extinguished in the cave-in. With the darkness
pushing in around me, the dust filling my lungs, it

was all I could do not to panic. I thought of Father and the story he always told of the cave-in of '33, back in Cornwall. Picturing his face, the black lines spreading out from his eyes when he told us those stories, his voice a whisper, then a boom, it calmed me, and I crawled on and found Maloney half buried, still swearing. Scooping the rocks and dirt out with my hands—Maloney helping with his free arm, all the time abusing me—I finally pulled him free. His left foot looked to be in a bad way. I hauled him back above ground, just as I have hauled him now from the Pick & Barrow. By his snoring, I doubt his foot is paining him much now.

    Today's close shave has made my mind up. I have been thinking about it for some time, ever since I abandoned my claim, but now I am decided—I am leaving the Ballarat. Truth be known, it is only stubborn pride that has kept me here this long; Mammy's words ringing in my empty head, "It's a big chance you're taking, risking your life, losing your loved ones, to chase a rainbow." Well, Mammy, my rainbow chasing days are over; I do not want to die in a dusty mine shaft. I am striking out for Melbourne town come morning.

28 November 1857

There is not the time to tell of all the sights I have seen these past five days. The excitement began not far from the diggings when a man on a horse galloped up to the cart I was riding on, yelling and waving his hands. I thought he was a bushranger, one of these high-way bandits that hold up coaches. It turned out his wife was giving birth in a camp close by and he was hoping one of us might be a doctor. All of us on the cart were only miners, though the fellow next to me said he had helped birth a calf once. Everyone laughed, and the worried father-to-be rode off in a cloud of dust.

Melbourne is growing apace. Whole city blocks, whole settlements, have shot up like spring grass since last I was here. I made my own camp a few miles up the river. Last night, lying in my tent, I heard this far off moaning sound and something going clack, clack, clack, like a clock keeping time. At first I thought the sounds must have been coming from another of the strange animals that inhabit these parts, but after a while, once I got my courage up, I looked out of the tent and saw the glow and shadows of a large fire burning further up the river bank. It was the Blacks, having some sort of ceremony. I crept towards them, crouching low, trying not to make a sound. The moaning noise seemed to be made by men blowing into thin, hollow logs and the clacking came from other men clapping sticks together. I watched for what must have been over an hour as they danced and stamped and sang wailing hymns to their pagan gods. Some were all but naked, covered in some sort of oil and dotted with what looked like white paint, while others, perhaps the older ones, wore long fur capes to protect them from the evening chill. I do not mind confessing, I found the whole affair quite fascinating. I was scared at first, but after a while, the fear left me. They knew I was there—everyone in the colony says you cannot creep up on a black man—but they let me watch regardless.

3 December 1857

I have been too exhausted to write. Life, it seems, is either too boring or too busy to write about. Of late, it has been too much the latter. I met a man named Wallace Taylor who said he could find me some work at the Port. For four days now we have been loading bales of wool onto schooners bound for home. To think I left the diggings because the work was too hard and dangerous! A man died at the Port last week, crushed by a pile of bales that collapsed in a ship's hull. If I was not so tired, or so proud, I might have hatched a plan by now to stowaway on one of these ships. I do miss my kith and kin so. I dream most every night of Mammy's stew and her great steaming puddings. What I would give to sup at her table this very night! Ah, but that is the price of adventure. Or so I tell myself.

5 December 1857

Not a stowaway, but the next best thing! The Captain of a schooner, the Margaret Nicol, has agreed to take me on as a deckhand. He has lost half his crew to the rumour of another strike up near Forest Creek. I thought of trying my luck there, too, but I have decided to put rainbows behind me for good and to swallow my pride and return to Falmouth. We set sail first light tomorrow and should be in England before Spring!

7 December 1857

I write now as a record, in case my luck continues on this wretched course and I am dead and someone later finds this journal and so will know my fate and that of my fellow crewmen. We put to sea two days ago under fine skies. We were not five leagues beyond Port Phillip Bay, though, when the winds picked up and dark clouds covered us. The Captain was experienced and seemed well in control, but it was all hands on deck throughout the day and into the night. The rumour was he planned to drop anchor on the leeward side of an island, to take shelter for the night, to see off the storm. The schooner lurched in all directions, tossed and blown like a leaf. I was trying to retie a rope on the mainsail when I heard a tremendous crash. It was as if the Heavens themselves had rent in two. If I had not been holding the rope, I would have been thrown overboard right there and then. As it was, I flew across the deck like a harpoon, jolting to a screaming stop when I reached the end of my tether. The noise was tremendous, like a giant grinding his teeth. The Margaret Nicol, it seems, had foundered on rock; her hull being gouged to pieces. Perhaps the bales plugged the hole, but for an eerie moment everything went silent and still. Then there was another wave, another enormous cracking of wood on rock, and the ship listed portside. I let go of the rope and slid across the deck, dangling from the gunwale. The last thing I remember clearly was my fingers clinging desperately to that worn, slippery wood.

The next few hours are blank pages in the book of my memory. I imagine I hit my head on the hull as I fell into the sea. Somehow, by some miracle, I landed, or in my senseless state, clambered upon the plank of wood that saved my life. I am no great swimmer, so it was only good fortune or the mercy of God that delivered me safely to land. It was still dark when I awoke, washed up upon a beach, the plank still beneath me; my self, a piece of driftwood. Though the storm had eased, the waves were still enormous, but ebbing, leaving me to this drier Fate. My head was cleft with pain, though I could find no blood. I dragged myself into the bushes above the sand and drifted on sleep—much as I had upon the storm's savage swell—until morning light.

I have spent these past hours scouring the shore for fellow survivors, collecting what flotsam had been washed up with me from the wreckage. The Margaret Nicol is completely sunk, and I can only guess at the rocks upon which she foundered. Alas, I seem to be the sole survivor. I did, though, find one of my fellow crewmen, Arnold Bailey—dead, his torso draped in seaweed, the birds already pecking at his remains. I dug him a resting place in the sand and hauled his waterlogged body, the flesh all blue and bloated, and eased him into his shallow grave. Saying the Lord's Prayer over his mound, I succumbed to feelings of desperate loneliness, to my fear and grief, and wept on Bailey's tomb like I were his own mother.

I did find some useful items washed up on the shoreline: 1 bottle of Sanderson's rum; 7 good lengths of planking (along with many shorter, broken pieces of lumber); a torn section of sail about the size of a large blanket; 3 tins of potted meat; and 1 empty mustard jar. I must also confess to stripping Bailey of his outer garments and of filching his good leather belt and the knife that hung from it. The bounty on my own person was less rewarding—1 kerchief; 1 pipe (stem broken); 1 pouch of sodden tobacco; 1 flint; and the key to my chest. It was, though, the discovery of this very book and pen in the inner pocket of my waistcoat that most gladdened my heart. I am not sure why. A form of companionship, perhaps? Regardless, it set me on a fool's errand, as I spent time that I should have used to find food, burning wood to make ink from charcoal and ground-up rock and water, which I now have captured in my mustard jar.

8 December 1957

The days are warm, but the nights, when the wind picks up, are cold. I have made a rough shelter in amongst some rocks from the planks and the branches of trees, but not it, nor the sail, nor Bailey's clothes could keep out the freezing wind.

Today I explored further afield and made the dismal discovery that I am tossed up upon an island. I have circumnavigated it now and have yet to find human habitation, though I found an old campfire on the western shore, close by some rock pools that offered me up a meal of mussels. The northern tip of the island is like a finger of land, pointing to the mainland, which is no more than a league or two across the sea. There is no sign of human habitation there either, though I thought I saw smoke in the far off distance. I expect there are tribes of natives living in that density of bush.

The middle of the island remains a mystery to me. Perhaps some natives live there, inland. I will explore it on the morrow. For now, I must make the most of the dwindling light and build a fire big enough to warm me through the night.

10 December 1857

I did not write yesterday from exhaustion. I traversed the island's blank interior. No sign of natives. I found a creek, more a runnel of water, and I spent today carrying my planks of wood and other precious possessions to the north western shore, where there

is water and I will be more sheltered from the wind.
I keep myself busy to ward off the loneliness, to keep
my panic at bay. I have only 1 tin of potted meat left.

11 December 1857

I spent all day trying to catch a fish, using Bailey's
bootlaces for a line and a bent nail from a plank
as a hook. I had 3 nibbles, but the rogues all took
my bait and beat a hasty retreat. At one point my
frustration became fury as I tossed the tackle into the
sea. Realising my folly, I quickly stripped myself bare
and dove in after it. I later found more mussels and
ate them, keeping the potted meat in reserve. I am
hungry all the time. My gut feels hollowed-out, the
morsels I drop in it echoing like a pebbles dropped
in a well. I am dizzy, too. Whenever I stand, my
head goes to sea. I flit back and forth from curses
to prayers; cursing my luck, praying it will change.
I picture Mammy and baby Ella (who is no more a
baby, I guess) and I weep.

15 December 1857

I have not written for fear of giving flight to
thoughts of despair. I spent all of one day hunting
gulls with a spear fashioned from Bailey's knife.
After hours of failed attempts, I winged one and

dove upon the wretch like the desperate dog I have become. The bird's flesh was tough and oily and sat like a slick on the shallow waters of my stomach. Still, I am sure it gave me strength.

That night, when the sun went down, it was as if it had set in my own fiery skin. My face and neck were badly burned, pulled tighter than a drum. I used the grease from the gull's carcass as a balm, and the next morning I was swarmed by flies. I laughed at that as I plunged into the ocean and washed away the flies, the gull grease, and scrubbed at my deeper fears.

17 December 1857

Today, the skin on my neck is coming off in strips. I have lost pounds of weight and my clothes are turning to rags. Yesterday, when I was looking for eggs among the cliffs on the eastern shore (no luck!), I saw a ship crawl across the far horizon. Of course, those on board could not see or hear me, but that did not stop me jumping up and down, waving my arms, yelling until I was hoarse. Watching that sloop dwindle from sight was a kind of death for me. But from that, my hope has been resurrected. I have decided that I must make it to the mainland. The distance is not great, and if I make a new shelter from branches and scrub, I think I can fashion some sort of raft from the Nicol's old planks. Perhaps I will drown, or I will make it to other side and find no human help, but at least it gives me a chance. Left here, I will starve, or go crazy with sorrow and despair.

20 December 1857

I think it is three days since last I wrote—I have been so busy making a new shelter and working on the raft that I have lost track. Binding the planks together is proving difficult. I have experimented with seaweed, but yesterday I found a long, tussocky grass that I think may be stronger. My hunting and fishing exploits continue to be more comical than nourishing. Two days ago, I did manage to catch a fish; though its tiny size made me think I should use it for bait to lure something more substantial. Then yesterday I spent a fruitless morning trying to trap green parrots with my newest invention, a bird net made of Bailey's trousers, the bottom of the legs tied closed. The problem was, the trousers filled with so much air that I could not propel the net fast enough to catch the birds. In the end, sitting despondently watching the birds as the taunted me, flitting from tree to tree, I observed that they were feasting on tiny red berries. So, instead of eating the parrots, I ate what the parrots were eating—berries. Unfortunately, my constitution is arranged along different lines than that of a green parrot, and I have been regularly squatting in the grass ever since!

Christmas Eve 1857

The raft is built. I am no shipwright, but I think it is sea-worthy enough to make the journey. It even has a mast, which I will have to hold in place, and the piece of sail from the Nicol will return to its original occupation. It is appropriate, given the date (if I have it right), that I feel the same nervous anticipation I used to feel as boy the night before Christmas. Of course, I know no Christmas pudding awaits me on that other shore, but . . . Ah, Mammy. I leave tomorrow, a short leg of a much longer voyage, which, in God I trust, will one day take me home.

Christmas Day 1857

I have both laughed and cried this morning. I seem to have lost yesterday's hope and optimism. When I awoke I was paralysed by the thought that even if I make the crossing, my plight on the mainland might be worse than it is here. At least here I have shelter, fresh water, and shell fish. Then a skiffle drifted across the coast, the raindrops barely touching the ground, and the sun came back out and with it a rainbow, one end of which hovered near the highest peak of the mountains on the mainland. I hooted like a madman. So, despite myself, it seems I am destined to chase rainbows, misty dreams, colours in the air.

I am taking my one remaining tin of potted meat with me (the bottle of Sanderson's rum was long ago drained), but I am leaving this journal, my most precious possession, here, as an act of faith that I will find truer companions on the other side, but also as insurance, in case I drown in the attempt. I will bury this in what's left of Bailey's shirt and hope that some day hence a visitor to this windswept rock will find it and will read this true account of the survival of me, Amos Boyle, Cornishman, son of a tin miner, chaser of rainbows.

I wish you well and my self, God's speed.

Original manuscript uncovered on Gabo Island, September 2007

ACKNOWLEDGEMENTS

Paul Ashton (period). He made it happen. Thanks.

www.ingramcontent.com/pod-product-compliance
Lightning Source LLC
Chambersburg PA
CBHW030457010526
44118CB00011B/988